Learning BOOTSTRAP
Easy Web App Development

By Michael Bohner

Copyright©2015 Michael Bohner

All Rights Reserved

Copyright © 2015 by Bohner M.

All rights reserved. No part of this publication may be reproduced, distributed, or transmitted in any form or by any means, including photocopying, recording, or other electronic or mechanical methods, without the prior written permission of the author, except in the case of brief quotations embodied in critical reviews and certain other noncommercial uses permitted by copyright law.

Table of Contents

Introduction

Chapter 1- Definition

Chapter 2- The Grid system in Bootstrap 3

Chapter 3- Bootstrap Typography/Text

   Browser vs. Bootstrap Defaults
   The "<dl>" element
   The "<code>" element
   The <pre> element
   Contextual Backgrounds and colors

Chapter 4- Images in Bootstrap

   Images with Rounded Corners
   Circular images
   Responsive images in Bootstrap
   Image Gallery
   Responsive Embeds

Chapter 5- Jumbotrons in Bootstrap

   Jumbotron inside Container
   Jumbotron outside the container
   Page Headers

Chapter 6- Wells in Bootstrap

Well size

Chapter 7- Alerts in Bootstrap

Closing Alerts

Animated Alerts

Chapter 8- Button Groups in Bootstrap

Vertical Button Groups

Justified Button Groups

Nesting of Dropdown & Menus Button Groups

Split Button Groups

Chapter 9- Glyphicons in Bootstrap

Chapter 10- Badges and Labels in Bootstrap

Badges

Labels

Chapter 11- Progress Bars in Bootstrap

Progress bar having a Label

Progress bars with colors

Progress Bars with stripes

Progress Bars with Animation

Stacked Progress Bars

Chapter 12- The Tooltip plugin in Bootstrap

Conclusion

Disclaimer

While all attempts have been made to verify the information provided in this book, the author does assume any responsibility for errors, omissions, or contrary interpretations of the subject matter contained within. **The information provided in this book is for educational and entertainment purposes only. The reader is responsible for his or her own actions and the author does not accept any responsibilities for any liabilities or damages, real or perceived, resulting from the use of this information.**

The trademarks that are used are without any consent, and the publication of the trademark is without permission or backing by the trademark owner. All trademarks and brands within this book are for clarifying purposes only and are the owned by the owners themselves, not affiliated with this document.

Introduction

The development of responsive web pages is one of the emerging trends and issues in the field of applications development. Bootstrap helps developers to easily implement these, and this book will guide you on how to do it.

Chapter 1- Definition

Recently, the Bootstrap development team released Bootstrap 3. It can be used for the development of responsive and mobile-first websites. Most of the current websites can only be opened in computers. Once one tries to open them on devices with small screens, such as tablets and mobile phones, their structure changes completely into an ugly appearance. Bootstrap solves this problem, as the web pages of your app will fit on all of the devices having different screen sizes.

In the first part of this book, you learned how to get started with Bootstrap. This involves downloading the files, and then setting them up ready for programming. If you do not know how to do this, kindly consult the first book, and all will be well. The file structure of Bootstrap files was also discussed, so you should be able to understand this. These will not be discussed in this second book, so familiarize yourself with them by reading the first volume of this book.

Note that the main aim of developing Bootstrap 3 was to make it easy for programmers to create mobile first websites. With this kind of websites or web pages, the pages will automatically adjust themselves so as to fit on the mobile device. Proper rendering and touch zooming will have been achieved.

Consider the example given below:

<!DOCTYPE html>

```html
<html lang="en">

<head>
  <title>Bootstrap page Example</title>

  <meta charset="utf-8">

  <meta name="viewport" content="width=device-width, initial-scale=1">

  <link rel="stylesheet" href="http://maxcdn.bootstrapcdn.com/bootstrap/3.3.5/css/bootstrap.min.css">

  <script src="https://ajax.googleapis.com/ajax/libs/jquery/1.11.3/jquery.min.js"></script>
```

```html
  <script src="http://maxcdn.bootstrapcdn.com/bootstrap/3.3.5/js/bootstrap.min.js"></script>

</head>

<body>

  <div class="container">

    <h1>This is a Bootstrap 3 page</h1>

    <p>The following is our text for the page.</p>

    <p>Bootstrap is an easy framework for us to learn and understand.</p>

  </div>
```

</body>

</html>

Just write the program, and then run it. You will observe the following output in the browser:

This is a Bootstrap 3 page

The following is our text for the page.

Bootstrap is an easy framework for us to learn and understand.

The above page is fully responsive and running it on devices with different screens will show no negative effect, but the page will automatically adjust itself so as to fit well. Note that in this case, we have not downloaded the Bootstrap files, but we are using them from the Content Delivery Network (CDN). This was discussed in the first volume of this book, so if you are not aware of it, just consult the book and all will be okay.

Chapter 2- The Grid system in Bootstrap 3

Note that there were not much change to the grid system of Bootstrap in Bootstrap 3 from the previous versions of the framework. With this framework, a maximum of 12 columns will be allowed or supported across a single page. However, this does not mean that all of the twelve columns must be used on each page. One can choose to combine them so that wider columns can be used. Note that these grids are responsible for the responsive nature of Bootstrap, and they automatically respond to the width of different devices.

The grid system of Bootstrap 3 utilizes four classes for the different devices. These are given below:

- Xs – this is for phones.

- sm – this is for tablets.

- md- this is for desktops.

- Lg- this is for larger desktops.

For one to create more flexible and dynamic web pages, the above classes can be combined together.

The following code shows the basic structure of the grid system in bootstrap 3:

```
<div class="row">

  <div class="col-*-*"></div>

</div>

<div class="row">

  <div class="col-*-*"></div>

  <div class="col-*-*"></div>
```

```
<div class="col-*-*"></div>

</div>

<div class="row">

...

</div>
```

Note that we have started by creating a *"div"* of class *"row,"* and then we have added the number of columns that we need. However, the numbers specified in ".col-*-*" when added up must give a result of 12. This is for each of the rows which you specify. Let us demonstrate this by use of an example:

```
<!DOCTYPE html>
<html lang="en">
<head>
<title>Bootstrap sample code </title>
```

```html
<meta charset="utf-8">
<meta name="viewport" content="width=device-width, initial-scale=1">
<link rel="stylesheet" href="http://maxcdn.bootstrapcdn.com/bootstrap/3.3.5/css/bootstrap.min.css">
<script src="https://ajax.googleapis.com/ajax/libs/jquery/1.11.3/jquery.min.js"></script>
<script src="http://maxcdn.bootstrapcdn.com/bootstrap/3.3.5/js/bootstrap.min.js"></script>
</head>
<body>
<div class="container-fluid">
<h1>Hello there!</h1>
<p>Try to resize the browser window and observe the effect.</p>
<div class="row">
<div class="col-sm-4" style="background-color:blue;">.col-sm-4</div>
```

```html
<div class="col-sm-4" style="background-color:yellow;">.col-sm-4</div>
<div class="col-sm-4" style="background-color:red;">.col-sm-4</div>
</div>
</div>
</body>
</html>
```

Just write the above program, and then open it in your browser. The following output will be observed from it:

What happened is that we have created 3 columns in our row. This explains the source of the colored columns in the output. Note that each of the columns has taken a width of 4, and they all add up to 12. This is how the grid system is used in Bootstrap 3.

Consider the example given below:

```html
<!DOCTYPE html>
<html lang="en">
<head>
<title>Bootstrap sample code</title>
<meta charset="utf-8">
<meta name="viewport" content="width=device-width, initial-scale=1">
<link rel="stylesheet" href="http://maxcdn.bootstrapcdn.com/bootstrap/3.3.5/css/bootstrap.min.css">
<script src="https://ajax.googleapis.com/ajax/libs/jquery/1.11.3/jquery.min.js"></script>
<script src="http://maxcdn.bootstrapcdn.com/bootstrap/3.3.5/js/bootstrap.min.js"></script>
</head>
<body>
<div class="container-fluid">
<h1>Hello there!</h1>
```

```
<p>Try to resize the browser window and observe the the effect.</p>
<div class="row">
<div class="col-sm-4" style="background-color:blue;">.col-sm-4</div>
<div class="col-sm-8" style="background-color:red;">.col-sm-8</div>
</div>
</div>
</body>
</html>
```

Just write the above program as it is, and then run it. You will observe the following output:

In the above example, we have created two columns in our row. However, the two columns are not of the same width. This is the feature which is commonly used on devices with smaller screens. One of the columns has a width of 4, while the other one has a width of 8, and the two add up to 12, which is okay.

Chapter 3- Bootstrap Typography/Text

With Bootstrap, the default setting for the text is that it should have a size of 14px, and a line-height of 1.428. Whenever you create your body and paragraphs in Bootstrap, this setting is applied to them. Also, all of the elements of the class "<p>"havea margin at the bottom of 10px by default.

Browser vs. Bootstrap Defaults

When you use the HTML headings with Bootstrap, they will be styled by default. The following code illustrates how this is done:

```
<!DOCTYPE html>
<html lang="en">
<head>
<title>Bootstrap sample code</title>
```

```html
<meta charset="utf-8">
<meta name="viewport" content="width=device-width, initial-scale=1">
<link rel="stylesheet" href="http://maxcdn.bootstrapcdn.com/bootstrap/3.3.5/css/bootstrap.min.css">
<script src="https://ajax.googleapis.com/ajax/libs/jquery/1.11.3/jquery.min.js"></script>
<script src="http://maxcdn.bootstrapcdn.com/bootstrap/3.3.5/js/bootstrap.min.js"></script>
</head>
<body>
<div class="container">
<h1>h1 heading in Bootstrap (36px)</h1>
<h2>h2 heading in Bootstrap (30px)</h2>
<h3>h3 heading in Bootstrap (24px)</h3>
<h4>h4 heading in Bootstrap (18px)</h4>
<h5>h5 heading in Bootstrap (14px)</h5>
<h6>h6 heading in Bootstrap (12px)</h6>
```

```
</div>
</body>
</html>
```

Just write the above program, and then run it. You will notice the following as its output:

h1 heading in Bootstrap (36px)
h2 heading in Bootstrap (30px)
h3 heading in Bootstrap (24px)
h4 heading in Bootstrap (18px)
h5 heading in Bootstrap (14px)
h6 heading in Bootstrap (12px)

As shown in the above figure, the headings have been formatted differently, depending on the type of heading which we have specified. This is how powerful Bootstrap is.

"<mark> style

When this style has been used, the contents will be styled as shown below:

```html
<!DOCTYPE html>
<html lang="en">
<head>
<title>Bootstrap Example</title>
<meta charset="utf-8">
<meta name="viewport" content="width=device-width, initial-scale=1">
<link rel="stylesheet" href="http://maxcdn.bootstrapcdn.com/bootstrap/3.3.5/css/bootstrap.min.css">
<script src="https://ajax.googleapis.com/ajax/libs/jquery/1.11.3/jquery.min.js"></script>
<script src="http://maxcdn.bootstrapcdn.com/bootstrap/3.3.5/js/bootstrap.min.js"></script>
</head>
<body>
<div class="container">
<h1>Highlighted Text</h1>
```

```
<p>the element mark is used to
<mark>highlight</mark> text.</p>
</div>


</body>
</html>
```

Just write the program as shown above, and then run it. You will observe the following output:

Highlighted Text
the element mark is used to highlight text.

As shown in the figure, the element in which we have used the tag has been marked. This shows the purpose of the tag.

<abbr> element

When this element has been used, the text is styled as shown in the example given below:

```html
<!DOCTYPE html>
<html lang="en">
<title>bootstrap sample code</title>
<meta charset="utf-8">
<meta name="viewport"
content="width=device-width, initial-scale=1">
<link rel="stylesheet" href="http://maxcdn.bootstrapcdn.com/bootstrap/3.3.5/css/bootstrap.min.css">
<script src="https://ajax.googleapis.com/ajax/libs/jquery/1.11.3/jquery.min.js"></script>
<script src="http://maxcdn.bootstrapcdn.com/bootstrap/3.3.5/js/bootstrap.min.js"></script>
</head>
<body>
<div class="container">
<h1>Abbreviations in Bootstrap 3</h1>
```

```html
<p>When this element is used, the text is marked as an acronym or an abbreviation:</p>
<p>The <abbr title="United States of America">USA</abbr> is headed by a President.</p>
</div>
</body>
</html>
```

`<blockquote>` element

When this element has been used, the text is changed to the following:

```html
<!DOCTYPE html>
<html lang="en">
<head>
<title>Bootstrap 3 sample code</title>
<meta charset="utf-8">
<meta name="viewport" content="width=device-width, initial-scale=1">
```

```html
<link rel="stylesheet" href="http://maxcdn.bootstrapcdn.com/bootstrap/3.3.5/css/bootstrap.min.css">
<script src="https://ajax.googleapis.com/ajax/libs/jquery/1.11.3/jquery.min.js"></script>
<script src="http://maxcdn.bootstrapcdn.com/bootstrap/3.3.5/js/bootstrap.min.js"></script>
</head>
<body>
<div class="container">
<h1>Blockquotes example</h1>
<p>The blockquote element is used for representation of text which is from another source:</p>
<blockquote>
```

```
<p> Note that there was not much change to the grid system of Bootstrap in Bootstrap 3 from the previous versions of the framework. With this framework, a maximum of 12 columns will be allowed or supported across a single page. However, this does not mean that all of the twelve columns must be used on each page. Once can choose to combine them so that wider columns can be used.</p>
<footer>From my Bootstrap book</footer>
</blockquote>
</div>
</body>
</html>
```

Just write the program as shown above, and then run it. You will observe the following as its output:

Blockquotes example

The blockquote element is used for representation of text which is from another source.

> Note that there were no much changes to the grid system of bootstrap in Bootstrap 3 from the previous versions of the framework. With this framework, a maximum of 12 columns will be allowed or supported across a single page. However, this does not mean that all of the twelve columns must be used on each page. Once can choose to combine them so that wider columns can be used.
>
> — From my Bootstrap book

As shown in the figure representing the output, the source of the text has been shown, and the user can easily understand what is happening.

The "<dl>" element

When this element has been used, the text is styled as follows:

```
<!DOCTYPE html>
<html lang="en">
<head>
<title>Bootstrap 3 sample code</title>
<meta charset="utf-8">
<meta name="viewport" content="width=device-width, initial-scale=1">
<link rel="stylesheet" href="http://maxcdn.bootstrapcdn.com/bootstrap/3.3.5/css/bootstrap.min.css">
```

```html
<script src="https://ajax.googleapis.com/ajax/libs/jquery/1.11.3/jquery.min.js"></script>
<script src="http://maxcdn.bootstrapcdn.com/bootstrap/3.3.5/js/bootstrap.min.js"></script>
</head>
<body>
<div class="container">
<h1>These are Description Lists</h1>
<p>The dl element is used to indicate that text is a description list:</p>
<dl>
<dt>John</dt>
<dd>- a famous athlete</dd>
<dt>Mercy</dt>
<dd>- Known for her humbleness</dd>
</dl>
</div>
</body>
</html>
```

Just write the above program as it is, and then run it. The following output will be observed:

These are Description Lists

The dl element is used to indicate that text is a description list:

John
- a famous athlete
Mercy
- Known for her humbleness

That is how the element can be used.

The "<code>" element

When this element is used, the text is styled as follows:

<!DOCTYPE html>
<html lang="en">
<head>
<title>Bootstrap sample code</title>
<meta charset="utf-8">

```html
<meta name="viewport" content="width=device-width, initial-scale=1">
<link rel="stylesheet" href="http://maxcdn.bootstrapcdn.com/bootstrap/3.3.5/css/bootstrap.min.css">
<script src="https://ajax.googleapis.com/ajax/libs/jquery/1.11.3/jquery.min.js"></script>
<script src="http://maxcdn.bootstrapcdn.com/bootstrap/3.3.5/js/bootstrap.min.js"></script>
</head>
<body>
<div class="container">
<h1>Code samples</h1>
<p>The code element is used to define inline snippets of code:</p>
```

```html
<p>The following examples of HTML elements: <code>span</code>, <code>section</code>, and <code>div</code> are used to define a section in a document.</p>
</div>
</body>
</html>
```

Just write the above program, and then run it. You will observe the following output:

Code samples

The code element is used to define inline snippets of code.

The following examples of HTML elements: `span`, `section`, and `div` are used to define a section in a document.

<kbd> element

When this element is used, the text is styled as shown below:

```
<!DOCTYPE html>
```

```html
<html lang="en">
<head>
<title>Bootstrap sample code</title>
<meta charset="utf-8">
<meta name="viewport" content="width=device-width, initial-scale=1">
<link rel="stylesheet" href="http://maxcdn.bootstrapcdn.com/bootstrap/3.3.5/css/bootstrap.min.css">
<script src="https://ajax.googleapis.com/ajax/libs/jquery/1.11.3/jquery.min.js"></script>
<script src="http://maxcdn.bootstrapcdn.com/bootstrap/3.3.5/js/bootstrap.min.js"></script>
</head>
<body>
<div class="container">
<h1>Sample Keyboard Inputs</h1>
```

```
<p>The kbd element is used to indicate that an element will be entered into the system via the kyboard:</p>
<p>Use <kbd>ctrl + c</kbd> to copy a text in a particular document.</p>
</div>
</body>
</html>
```

Just write the program as shown above, and then run it. You will observe the following as the output:

Sample Keyboard Inputs

The kbd element is used to indicate that an element will be entered into the system via the kyboard.

Use `ctrl + c` to copy a text in a particular document.

The <pre> element

When this element is used, the text will be styled as follows:

```
<!DOCTYPE html>
```

```html
<html lang="en">
<head>
<title>Bootstrap sample code</title>
<meta charset="utf-8">
<meta name="viewport" content="width=device-width, initial-scale=1">
<link rel="stylesheet" href="http://maxcdn.bootstrapcdn.com/bootstrap/3.3.5/css/bootstrap.min.css">
<script src="https://ajax.googleapis.com/ajax/libs/jquery/1.11.3/jquery.min.js"></script>
<script src="http://maxcdn.bootstrapcdn.com/bootstrap/3.3.5/js/bootstrap.min.js"></script>
</head>
<body>
<div class="container">
<h1>Multiple lines of code</h1>
<p>If you have multiple lines of code, the pre element can be used:</p>
```

```
<pre>
Text which has been written in the pre element
Will be displayed in a fixed-width
font, and it will preserves
both the     spaces and the
line breaks.
</pre>
</div>
</body>
</html>
```

Just write the above program, and then run it. You will observe the following output:

Multiple lines of code

If you have multiple lines of code, the pre element can be used:

```
Text which has been written in the pre element
Will be displayed in a fixed-width
font, and it will preserves
both the     spaces and the
line breaks.
```

Contextual Backgrounds and colors

With Bootstrap 3, there are some classes which can be provided for provision of some meaningful colors. These classes are shown in the example given below:

```
<!DOCTYPE html>
<html lang="en">
<head>
<title> Bootstrap sample code </title>
<meta charset="utf-8">
<meta name="viewport" content="width=device-width, initial-scale=1">
<link rel="stylesheet" href="http://maxcdn.bootstrapcdn.com/bootstrap/3.3.5/css/bootstrap.min.css">
<script src="https://ajax.googleapis.com/ajax/libs/jquery/1.11.3/jquery.min.js"></script>
<script src="http://maxcdn.bootstrapcdn.com/bootstrap/3.3.5/js/bootstrap.min.js"></script>
```

```html
</head>
<body>
<div class="container">
<h2>Contextual Colors in Bootstrap 3</h2>
<p>Use the contextual classes to provide "meaning through colors":</p>
<p class="text-muted">This text is muted.</p>
<p class="text-primary">This text is important.</p>
<p class="text-success">This text indicates success.</p>
<p class="text-info">This text represents some information.</p>
<p class="text-warning">This text represents a warning.</p>
<p class="text-danger">This text represents danger.</p>
</div>
</body>
</html>
```

Just write the above program, and then run it. You will observe the following as the output from it:

Bootstrap Contextual Colors

Bootstrap contextual classes can be used for provision of "meaning through colors":

This text has been muted.

This text is important.

This text is an indication of success.

This text is a representation of some information.

This text is a representation of a warning.

This text is a representation of danger.

The following example illustrates how background colors can be used:

<!DOCTYPE html>
<html lang="en">
<head>
<title>Bootstrap 3 sample code</title>
<meta charset="utf-8">
<meta name="viewport" content="width=device-width, initial-scale=1">

```html
<link rel="stylesheet" href="http://maxcdn.bootstrapcdn.com/bootstrap/3.3.5/css/bootstrap.min.css">
<script src="https://ajax.googleapis.com/ajax/libs/jquery/1.11.3/jquery.min.js"></script>
<script src="http://maxcdn.bootstrapcdn.com/bootstrap/3.3.5/js/bootstrap.min.js"></script>
</head>
<body>
<div class="container">
<h2>Bootstrap 3 Contextual Backgrounds</h2>
<p>Contextual Backgrounds can be used for provision of "meaning through colors":</p>
<p class="bg-primary">This text is important.</p>
<p class="bg-success">This text is an indication of success.</p>
<p class="bg-info">This text is a representation of some information.</p>
```

```html
<p class="bg-warning">This text is a representation of a warning.</p>
<p class="bg-danger">This text is a representation of danger.</p>
</div>
</body>
</html>
```

Just write the program, and then run it. You will observe the following as the output:

Bootstrap 3 Contextual Backgrounds

Contextual Backgrounds can be used for provision of "meaning through colors":

This text is important.

This text is an indication of success.

This text is a representation of some information.

This text is a representation of a warning.

This text is a representation of danger.

Chapter 4- Images in Bootstrap

In Bootstrap, images can be specified, but in different shapes. Some can have rounded corners, while others can have sharp corners. This is what we will discuss in this chapter.

Images with Rounded Corners

For us to create images whose corners are rounded, we use the class ".img-rounded."An example of this is given below:

```
<!DOCTYPE html>
<html lang="en">
<head>
<title>Bootstrap 3 sample code</title>
<meta charset="utf-8">
```

```html
<meta name="viewport" content="width=device-width, initial-scale=1">
<link rel="stylesheet" href="http://maxcdn.bootstrapcdn.com/bootstrap/3.3.5/css/bootstrap.min.css">
<script src="https://ajax.googleapis.com/ajax/libs/jquery/1.11.3/jquery.min.js"></script>
<script src="http://maxcdn.bootstrapcdn.com/bootstrap/3.3.5/js/bootstrap.min.js"></script>
</head>
<body>
<div class="container">
<h2>Image with Rounded Corners</h2>
<p>The class .img-rounded is used to add rounded corners to an image:</p>
<imgsrc="img.jpg" class="img-rounded" alt="My image" width="304" height="236">
</div>
</body>
```

</html>

Just write the program as it is shown above, and then run it. The following output will be observed:

As shown in the above figure, the corners of the image are rounded. That is how the class can be used, and it offers a very interesting feature.

Circular images

In this case, we use the class "*.img-circle*" so as to get a circular image. You need to note thatIE8 does not support a circular image.

```
<!DOCTYPE html>
<html lang="en">
<head>
<title>Bootstrap sample code</title>
<meta charset="utf-8">
<meta name="viewport" content="width=device-width, initial-scale=1">
<link rel="stylesheet" href="http://maxcdn.bootstrapcdn.com/bootstrap/3.3.5/css/bootstrap.min.css">
<script src="https://ajax.googleapis.com/ajax/libs/jquery/1.11.3/jquery.min.js"></script>
<script src="http://maxcdn.bootstrapcdn.com/bootstrap/3.3.5/js/bootstrap.min.js"></script>
</head>
```

```html
<body>
<div class="container">
<h2>Circular image in Bootstrap</h2>
<p>The class .img-circle is used to shapean image into a circle (note that it is not available in IE8):</p>
<imgsrc="img.jpg" class="img-circle" alt="My image" width="304" height="236">
</div>
</body>
</html>
```

You can write the above program and then run it. You will get the following as the output:

Thumbnail

In this case, we use the class ".img-thumbnail" so as to shape an image into a thumbnail. Consider the example given below:

```
<!DOCTYPE html>
<html lang="en">
<head>
<title>Bootstrap sample code</title>
<meta charset="utf-8">
<meta name="viewport" content="width=device-width, initial-scale=1">
<link rel="stylesheet" href="http://maxcdn.bootstrapcdn.com/bootstrap/3.3.5/css/bootstrap.min.css">
<script src="https://ajax.googleapis.com/ajax/libs/jquery/1.11.3/jquery.min.js"></script>
```

```
<script src="http://maxcdn.bootstrapcdn.com/bootstrap/3.3.5/js/bootstrap.min.js"></script>
</head>
<body>
<div class="container">
<h2>Bootstrap Thumbnail image</h2>
<p>The class .img-thumbnail is used to create a thumbnail of an image:</p>
<imgsrc="img.jpg" class="img-thumbnail" alt="My image" width="304" height="236">
</div>
</body>
</html>
```

You can write the above program as it is, and then run it. The following will be observed as the output:

Bootstrap Thumbnail image

The class .img-thumbnail is used to create a thumbnail of an image:

Responsive images in Bootstrap

Images are of different sizes. The same case applies to device screens. When images are declared as responsive, one will have no problem in rendering images on screens of different sizes.

To create responsive images in Bootstrap, the class ".img-responsive" is added to the tag "<img>."When this is done, the image will scale very well so as to fit the parent screen. When this has been set, the property *"max-width"* will be set to 100%, and the property *"height"* will be set to *"auto."* Consider the example given below:

```html
<!DOCTYPE html>
<html lang="en">
<head>
<title>Bootstrap sample code</title>
<meta charset="utf-8">
<meta name="viewport" content="width=device-width, initial-scale=1">
<link rel="stylesheet" href="http://maxcdn.bootstrapcdn.com/bootstrap/3.3.5/css/bootstrap.min.css">
<script src="https://ajax.googleapis.com/ajax/libs/jquery/1.11.3/jquery.min.js"></script>
<script src="http://maxcdn.bootstrapcdn.com/bootstrap/3.3.5/js/bootstrap.min.js"></script>
</head>
<body>
<div class="container">
<h2>Responsive Image</h2>
```

```html
<p>The class .img-responsive will make your image scale well to the parent element (try to resize the browser window and observe the effect):</p>
<img class="img-responsive" src="img.jpg" alt="My image" width="460" height="345">
</div>
</body>
</html>
```

Just write the above program, and then run it. You will observe the following as the output:

Note the case which is shown above. I have minimized the browser so as to get my image. That is how it will appear on devices with small screens, such as mobile phones and tablets.

Image Gallery

One can take advantage of the class ".thumbnail" and the Bootstrap grid system so as to create an image gallery. An example of this is given below:

```html
<!DOCTYPE html>
<html lang="en">
<head>
<title>Bootstrap sample code</title>
<meta charset="utf-8">
<meta name="viewport" content="width=device-width, initial-scale=1">
<link rel="stylesheet" href="http://maxcdn.bootstrapcdn.com/bootstrap/3.3.5/css/bootstrap.min.css">
<script src="https://ajax.googleapis.com/ajax/libs/jquery/1.11.3/jquery.min.js"></script>
<script src="http://maxcdn.bootstrapcdn.com/bootstrap/3.3.5/js/bootstrap.min.js"></script>
</head>
<body>
<div class="container">
<h2>Image Gallery in Bootstrap</h2>
```

```html
<p>The class.thumbnailcan be used for displaying an image gallery. Click on any of the images to observe it in full size:</p>
<div class="row">
<div class="col-md-4">
<a href="img.jpg" class="thumbnail">
<p>This is just a simple image. It has been used to demonstrate a gallery in bootstrap</p>
<imgsrc="img1.jpg" alt="Image 1" style="width:150px;height:150px">
</a>
</div>
<div class="col-md-4">
<a href="img2.jpg" class="thumbnail">
<p>This is just a simple image. It has been used to demonstrate a gallery in bootstrap.</p>
<imgsrc="img3.jpg" alt="Image 3" style="width:150px;height:150px">
</a>
</div>
```

```
<div class="col-md-4">
<a href="img2.jpg" class="thumbnail">
<p>The Cinque Terre: A rugged portion of coast in the Liguria region of Italy.</p>
<imgsrc="img3.jpg" alt="Cinque Terre" style="width:150px;height:150px">
</a>
</div>
</div>
</div>
</body>
</html>
```

Just write the program as it has been written above, and then run it. Be sure to observe the output that you get, and it should be as follows:

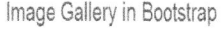

  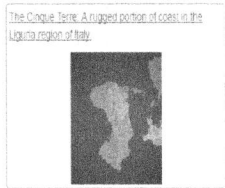

Responsive Embeds

Videos and slide shows which have been used on your website should be allowed to scale effectively. This should be the case on any device having a different screen.

Suppose you need to add a video to your code and then make it responsive. This can be done by adding the class ".embed-responsive-item" to the tag "<iframe>."When this is done, the video will be in a position to scale well on a device of any screen size. The definition of the aspect ratio of the video will be done within the "<div>" element.

Consider the following example, which shows how this can be done:

```
<!DOCTYPE html>
<html lang="en">
<head>
<title>Bootstrap sample code</title>
```

```html
<meta charset="utf-8">
<meta name="viewport" content="width=device-width, initial-scale=1">
<link rel="stylesheet" href="http://maxcdn.bootstrapcdn.com/bootstrap/3.3.5/css/bootstrap.min.css">
<script src="https://ajax.googleapis.com/ajax/libs/jquery/1.11.3/jquery.min.js"></script>
<script src="http://maxcdn.bootstrapcdn.com/bootstrap/3.3.5/js/bootstrap.min.js"></script>
</head>
<body>
<div class="container">
<h2>A Responsive Embed element</h2>
<div class="embed-responsive embed-responsive-16by9">
<iframe class="embed-responsive-item" src="http://www.youtube.com/embed/XFSz3_Czz8k"></iframe>
```

</div>
</div>
</body>
</html>

Just write the above program, and then run it. The following output will be observed from the program:

As shown in the above figure, the video has been obtained from YouTube. This is the URL which we have specified. In case you want to add a particular video to your website, this is how it can be done, and it can also be made responsive.

One can also opt to choose from the two classes of aspect ratio as shown below:

```html
<!-- 16:9 aspect ratio -->
<div class="embed-responsive embed-responsive-16by9">
  <iframe class="embed-responsive-item" src="..."></iframe>
</div>
<!-- 4:3 aspect ratio -->
<div class="embed-responsive embed-responsive-4by3">
  <iframe class="embed-responsive-item" src="..."></iframe>
</div>
```

Chapter 5- Jumbotrons in Bootstrap

Sometimes, one can need to attract attention from the readers of the website. In this case, a jumbotron can be used, which is a large and special box which is solely used for this. The displaying of this is done as a large box whose corners are round, and it is grey in color. The font size of the text displayed in it is also enlarged. Note that inside a jumbotron, one can add any elements such as the HTML ones and others belonging to Bootstrap.

To create a jumbotron, we use the <div> element together with the class ".jumbotron."

Jumbotron inside Container

In case you do not want your jumbotron to extend to the edge of your screen, the jumbotron can be placed inside the element "<div class="container">." Consider the example given below:

```html
<!DOCTYPE html>
<html lang="en">
<head>
<title>Bootstrap sample code</title>
<meta charset="utf-8">
<meta name="viewport" content="width=device-width, initial-scale=1">
<link rel="stylesheet" href="http://maxcdn.bootstrapcdn.com/bootstrap/3.3.5/css/bootstrap.min.css">
<script src="https://ajax.googleapis.com/ajax/libs/jquery/1.11.3/jquery.min.js"></script>
<script src="http://maxcdn.bootstrapcdn.com/bootstrap/3.3.5/js/bootstrap.min.js"></script>
</head>
<body>
<div class="container">
<div class="jumbotron">
```

```html
<h1>Jumbotron in Bootstrap</h1>
<p>the displaying of this is done as a large box whose corners are round, and it is grey in color. The font size of the text displayed in it is also enlarged.</p>
</div>
<p>This is a sample text.</p>
<p>This is another sample text.</p>
</div>
</body>
</html>
```

Just write the program as it is, and then run it. The following output will be observed:

Jumbotron in Bootstrap

the displaying of this is done as a large box whose corners are round, and it is grey in color. The font size of the text displayed in it is also enlarged.

This is a sample text.

This is another sample text.

Jumbotron outside the container

In case you need your jumbotron to extend to the edges of the screen of the device, the jumbotron can be placed outside the "<div class="container">" element. Consider the example given below:

```html
<!DOCTYPE html>
<html lang="en">
<head>
<title>Bootstrap sample code</title>
<meta charset="utf-8">
<meta name="viewport" content="width=device-width, initial-scale=1">
<link rel="stylesheet" href="http://maxcdn.bootstrapcdn.com/bootstrap/3.3.5/css/bootstrap.min.css">
<script src="https://ajax.googleapis.com/ajax/libs/jquery/1.11.3/jquery.min.js"></script>
```

```
<script src="http://maxcdn.bootstrapcdn.com/bootstrap/3.3.5/js/bootstrap.min.js"></script>
</head>
<body>
<div class="jumbotron">
<h1>Jumbotron in Bootstrap </h1>
<p> the displaying of this is done as a large box whose corners are round, and it is grey in color. The font size of the text displayed in it is also enlarged.</p>
</div>
<div class="container">
<p>This is some sample text.</p>
<p>This is another sample text.</p>
</div>
</body>
</html>
```

Just write the above program as it has been written, and then run it. You can then run it, and you will observe the following output:

Jumbotron in Bootstrap

the displaying of this is done as a large box whose corners are round, and it is grey in color. The font size of the text displayed in it is also enlarged.

This is some sample text

This is another sample text

Page Headers

This one will act just like a section divider. What happens is that we use the class ".page-header" which adds a horizontal line under the heading. Consider the example given below:

<!DOCTYPE html>
<html lang="en">
<head>
<title>Bootstrap sample code</title>
<meta charset="utf-8">

```html
<meta name="viewport" content="width=device-width, initial-scale=1">
<link rel="stylesheet" href="http://maxcdn.bootstrapcdn.com/bootstrap/3.3.5/css/bootstrap.min.css">
<script src="https://ajax.googleapis.com/ajax/libs/jquery/1.11.3/jquery.min.js"></script>
<script src="http://maxcdn.bootstrapcdn.com/bootstrap/3.3.5/js/bootstrap.min.js"></script>
</head>
<body>
<div class="container">
<div class="page-header">
<h1>A sample Page Header</h1>
</div>
<p>This is a sample text.</p>
<p>This is another sample text.</p>
</div>
</body>
```

`</html>`

Just write the program as it has been written above, and then run it. The following output will be observed from it:

A sample Page Header

This is a sample text.

This is another sample text.

Chapter 6- Wells in Bootstrap

With wells in Bootstrap, a rounded corner and a gray background is added to our element. Some padding is also added to the element. In this case, we use the class ".*well.*"Consider the example given below:

```
<!DOCTYPE html>
<html lang="en">
<head>
<title>Bootstrap Wells</title>
<meta charset="utf-8">
<meta name="viewport" content="width=device-width, initial-scale=1">
<link rel="stylesheet" href="http://maxcdn.bootstrapcdn.com/bootstrap/3.3.5/css/bootstrap.min.css">
<script src="https://ajax.googleapis.com/ajax/libs/jquery/1.11.3/jquery.min.js"></script>
```

```html
<script src="http://maxcdn.bootstrapcdn.com/bootstrap/3.3.5/js/bootstrap.min.js"></script>
</head>
<body>
<div class="container">
<h2>A Well example</h2>
<div class="well"> A Basic Well</div>
</div>
</body>
</html>
```

Just write the program as it is, and then run it. The following output will be observed:

A Well example

A Basic Well

Well size

Wells are different size and they can be of a small, medium, or large size. To create a small well, we use the class ".well-sm" while to create a large well, we use the class ".well-lg."Consider the example given below:

```
<!DOCTYPE html>
<html lang="en">
<head>
<title>Bootstrap sample code</title>
<meta charset="utf-8">
<meta name="viewport" content="width=device-width, initial-scale=1">
<link rel="stylesheet" href="http://maxcdn.bootstrapcdn.com/bootstrap/3.3.5/css/bootstrap.min.css">
<script src="https://ajax.googleapis.com/ajax/libs/jquery/1.11.3/jquery.min.js"></script>
```

```html
<script src="http://maxcdn.bootstrapcdn.com/bootstrap/3.3.5/js/bootstrap.min.js"></script>
</head>
<body>
<div class="container">
<h2>Size of a Well</h2>
<div class="well well-sm">A Small Well</div>
<div class="well">A Normal Well</div>
<div class="well well-lg">A Large Well</div>
</div>
</body>
</html>
```

Just write the program as it has been written above, and then run it. You will observe the following output:

Size of a Well

A Small Well

A Normal Well

A Large Well

Chapter 7- Alerts in Bootstrap

There are numerous ways that one can create alerts in Bootstrap. These alerts can illustrate a warning, a success, an error, or even important information. To do this, we use the class ".alert," and it is after this that we can specify the type of alert that we are creating. Consider the example given below:

```html
<!DOCTYPE html>
<html lang="en">
<head>
<title>Bootstrap sample code</title>
<meta charset="utf-8">
<meta name="viewport" content="width=device-width, initial-scale=1">
<link rel="stylesheet" href="http://maxcdn.bootstrapcdn.com/bootstrap/3.3.5/css/bootstrap.min.css">
```

```html
<script src="https://ajax.googleapis.com/ajax/libs/jquery/1.11.3/jquery.min.js"></script>
<script src="http://maxcdn.bootstrapcdn.com/bootstrap/3.3.5/js/bootstrap.min.js"></script>
</head>
<body>
<div class="container">
<h2>Alerts in Bootstrap</h2>
<div class="alert alert-success">
<strong>Success!</strong> This alert box is used to indicate a successful or positive action.
</div>
<div class="alert alert-info">
<strong>Info!</strong> This alert box is used to indicate a neutral informative change or an action.
</div>
<div class="alert alert-warning">
```

```html
<strong>Warning!</strong> This alert box is used to indicate a warning which might need some attention.
</div>
<div class="alert alert-danger">
<strong>Danger!</strong> This alert box is used to indicate a dangerous or a potentially negative action.
</div>
</div>
</body>
</html>
```

You can write the above program as it has been written, and then run it. You will then observe the following output:

Alerts in Bootstrap

Success! This alert box is used to indicate a successful or positive action.

Info! This alert box is used to indicate a neutral informative change or an action.

Warning! This alert box is used to indicate a warning which might need some attention.

Danger! This alert box is used to indicate a dangerous or a potentially negative action.

As shown in the above figure representing the output from the program, the alerts take a different color. For example, the red color has been used to indicate danger as usual.

Closing Alerts

If you want to be able to close the alert, the element "class="close"" or "data-dismiss="alert"" can be added to a button or a link element in the alert. This will definitely close the alert. An example of this is given below:

```html
<!DOCTYPE html>
<html lang="en">
<head>
<title>Bootstrap sample code</title>
<meta charset="utf-8">
<meta name="viewport" content="width=device-width, initial-scale=1">
<link rel="stylesheet" href="http://maxcdn.bootstrapcdn.com/bootstrap/3.3.5/css/bootstrap.min.css">
<script src="https://ajax.googleapis.com/ajax/libs/jquery/1.11.3/jquery.min.js"></script>
<script src="http://maxcdn.bootstrapcdn.com/bootstrap/3.3.5/js/bootstrap.min.js"></script>
</head>
<body>
<div class="container">
<h2>Alerts in Bootstrap</h2>
```

```html
<p>The a element with class="close" and data-dismiss="alert" is used to close the alert box.</p>
<div class="alert alert-success">
<a href="#" class="close" data-dismiss="alert" aria-label="close">&times;</a>
<strong>Success!</strong>This alert box is used to indicate a successful or positive action.
</div>
<div class="alert alert-info">
<a href="#" class="close" data-dismiss="alert" aria-label="close">&times;</a>
<strong>Info!</strong>This alert box is used to indicate a neutral informative change or an action.
</div>
<div class="alert alert-warning">
```

```html
    <a href="#" class="close" data-dismiss="alert" aria-label="close">&times;</a>
    <strong>Warning!</strong>This alert box is used to indicate a warning which might need some attention.
  </div>
  <div class="alert alert-danger">
    <a href="#" class="close" data-dismiss="alert" aria-label="close">&times;</a>
    <strong>Danger!</strong>This alert box is used to indicate a dangerous or a potentially negative action.
  </div>
</div>
</body>
</html>
```

Just write the program as it has been written above, and then run it. The following output will be observed:

Alerts in Bootstrap

The a element with class="close" and data-dismiss="alert" is used to close the alert box.

Success! This alert box is used to indicate a successful or positive action.

Info! This alert box is used to indicate a neutral informative change or an action.

Warning! This alert box is used to indicate a warning which might need some attention.

Danger! This alert box is used to indicate a dangerous or a potentially negative action.

You can click on the symbol "x" located at the right end of the alert, and then observe what happens. It will be closed. This is how a close button can be added to the alert dialog in Bootstrap. If you click on this symbol for all of the dialogs, they will all be closed.

Animated Alerts

In this case, we use the classes ".*in*" and ".*fade*" so as to add a fading effect to our alert while we are closing it. Consider the example given below:

<!DOCTYPE html>
<html lang="en">

```html
<head>
<title>Bootstrap sample code</title>
<meta charset="utf-8">
<meta name="viewport" content="width=device-width, initial-scale=1">
<link rel="stylesheet" href="http://maxcdn.bootstrapcdn.com/bootstrap/3.3.5/css/bootstrap.min.css">
<script src="https://ajax.googleapis.com/ajax/libs/jquery/1.11.3/jquery.min.js"></script>
<script src="http://maxcdn.bootstrapcdn.com/bootstrap/3.3.5/js/bootstrap.min.js"></script>
</head>
<body>
<div class="container">
<h2>Alerts in Bootstrap</h2>
<p>Theclasses  .fade and .in are used to add a fading effect when the alert message is being closed.</p>
```

```html
<div class="alert alert-success fade in">
<a href="#" class="close" data-dismiss="alert" aria-label="close">&times;</a>
<strong>Success!</strong>This alert box is used to indicate a successful or positive action.
</div>
<div class="alert alert-info fade in">
<a href="#" class="close" data-dismiss="alert" aria-label="close">&times;</a>
<strong>Info!</strong>This alert box is used to indicate a neutral informative change or an action.
</div>
<div class="alert alert-warning fade in">
<a href="#" class="close" data-dismiss="alert" aria-label="close">&times;</a>
```

```html
<strong>Warning!</strong>This alert box is used to indicate a warning which might need some attention.
</div>
<div class="alert alert-danger fade in">
<a href="#" class="close" data-dismiss="alert" aria-label="close">&times;</a>
<strong>Danger!</strong>This alert box is used to indicate a dangerous or a potentially negative action.
</div>
</div>
</body>
</html>
```

Just write the above program as it is, and then run it. The following output will be observed:

Alerts in Bootstrap

The classes fade and in are used to add a fading effect when the alert message is being closed.

Success! This alert box is used to indicate a successful or positive action.

Info! This alert box is used to indicate a neutral informative change or an action.

Warning! This alert box is used to indicate a warning which might need some attention.

Danger! This alert box is used to indicate a dangerous or a potentially negative action.

You can now try to close any of the alerts, and then observe how it exits. You will notice that an animation effect has been added to them.

Chapter 8- Button Groups in Bootstrap

This feature allows the users of Bootstrap to group more than one button together. In this case, the element "<div>" is used together with the class ".btn-group."

Consider the example given below:

```
<!DOCTYPE html>
<html lang="en">
<head>
<title>Bootstrap sample code</title>
<meta charset="utf-8">
<meta name="viewport" content="width=device-width, initial-scale=1">
<link rel="stylesheet" href="http://maxcdn.bootstrapcdn.com/bootstrap/3.3.5/css/bootstrap.min.css">
```

```html
<script src="https://ajax.googleapis.com/ajax/libs/jquery/1.11.3/jquery.min.js"></script>
<script src="http://maxcdn.bootstrapcdn.com/bootstrap/3.3.5/js/bootstrap.min.js"></script>
</head>
<body>

<div class="container">
<h2> A Button Group</h2>
<div class="btn-group">
<button type="button" class="btnbtn-primary">Android</button>
<button type="button" class="btnbtn-primary">Linux</button>
<button type="button" class="btnbtn-primary">OS X</button>
</div>
</div>
</body>
</html>
```

Just write the above program as it is, and then run it. You will observe the following as the output:

A Button Group with Android, Linux, OS X buttons

The figure shows that the three buttons have been grouped together to form a single button. However, the different buttons forming the button group can easily be differentiated.

It is possible for one to apply size to each of the buttons contained in the button group. However, it is easy for you to specify a particular size to be applied by all of the buttons contained in the button group. This can be done as shown in the example below:

<!DOCTYPE html>

```html
<html lang="en">
<head>
<title>Bootstrap sample code</title>
<meta charset="utf-8">
<meta name="viewport" content="width=device-width, initial-scale=1">
<link rel="stylesheet" href="http://maxcdn.bootstrapcdn.com/bootstrap/3.3.5/css/bootstrap.min.css">
<script src="https://ajax.googleapis.com/ajax/libs/jquery/1.11.3/jquery.min.js"></script>
<script src="http://maxcdn.bootstrapcdn.com/bootstrap/3.3.5/js/bootstrap.min.js"></script>
</head>
<body>
<div class="container">
<h2>Setting the size of Button Groups </h2>
```

```html
<p>This can be done by adding the class .btn-group-* to size all the buttons in the button group.</p>
<h3>Large Buttons:</h3>
<div class="btn-group btn-group-lg">
<button type="button" class="btnbtn-primary">Windows</button>
<button type="button" class="btnbtn-primary">Linux</button>
<button type="button" class="btnbtn-primary">OS X</button>
</div>
<h3>Extra Small Buttons:</h3>
<div class="btn-group btn-group-xs">
<button type="button" class="btnbtn-primary">Windows</button>
<button type="button" class="btnbtn-primary">Linux</button>
<button type="button" class="btnbtn-primary">OS X</button>
</div>
</div>
```

</body>
</html>

Just write the program as it has been written above, and then run it. The following output will be observed from it:

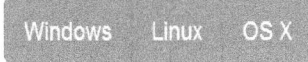

Notice how the buttons have maintained a uniform size. The size for each of the button groups has been set once, rather than setting each for an individual button.

Vertical Button Groups

With Bootstrap, button groups which are aligned vertically are supported. The class ".btn-group-vertical" is used for this purpose. Consider the example given below, which shows how this can be done:

```html
<!DOCTYPE html>
<html lang="en">
<head>
<title>Bootstrap sample code</title>
<meta charset="utf-8">
<meta name="viewport" content="width=device-width, initial-scale=1">
<link rel="stylesheet" href="http://maxcdn.bootstrapcdn.com/bootstrap/3.3.5/css/bootstrap.min.css">
<script src="https://ajax.googleapis.com/ajax/libs/jquery/1.11.3/jquery.min.js"></script>
```

```html
<script src="http://maxcdn.bootstrapcdn.com/bootstrap/3.3.5/js/bootstrap.min.js"></script>
</head>
<body>
<div class="container">
<h2>A Vertical Button Group</h2>
<div class="btn-group-vertical">
<button type="button" class="btnbtn-primary">Windows</button>
<button type="button" class="btnbtn-primary">Linux</button>
<button type="button" class="btnbtn-primary">OS X</button>
</div>
</div>
</body>
</html>
```

Just write the above program as it has been written, and then run it. Observe the output that you get, and this should be as follows:

A Vertical Button Group

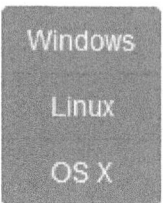

Justified Button Groups

These aRE button groups which span the entire length of your device screen. These can be created by use of the class ".btn-group-justified." Consider the example given below, which shows how these can be implemented with Bootstrap:

```
<!DOCTYPE html>
<html lang="en">
<head>
<title>Bootstrap sample code</title>
<meta charset="utf-8">
```

```html
<meta name="viewport" content="width=device-width, initial-scale=1">
<link rel="stylesheet" href="http://maxcdn.bootstrapcdn.com/bootstrap/3.3.5/css/bootstrap.min.css">
<script src="https://ajax.googleapis.com/ajax/libs/jquery/1.11.3/jquery.min.js"></script>
<script src="http://maxcdn.bootstrapcdn.com/bootstrap/3.3.5/js/bootstrap.min.js"></script>
</head>
<body>
<div class="container">
<h2>Justified Button Groups in Bootstrap</h2>
<div class="btn-group btn-group-justified">
<a href="#" class="btnbtn-primary">Windows</a>
<a href="#" class="btnbtn-primary">Linux</a>
```

```
<a href="#" class="btnbtn-primary">OS X</a>
    </div>
  </div>
</body>
</html>
```

Just write the above program as it has been written, and then run it. The output observed should be as follows:

As shown in the above figure, the width of the button group has spanned the entire width of the device screen. This is how this feature can be implemented with Bootstrap. Note that in the above case, we have used the elements with the tag "<a>."

For elements with the tag "<button>," this feature can be implemented as follows:

```html
<!DOCTYPE html>
<html lang="en">
<head>
<title>Bootstrap sample code</title>
<meta charset="utf-8">
<meta name="viewport" content="width=device-width, initial-scale=1">
<link rel="stylesheet" href="http://maxcdn.bootstrapcdn.com/bootstrap/3.3.5/css/bootstrap.min.css">
<script src="https://ajax.googleapis.com/ajax/libs/jquery/1.11.3/jquery.min.js"></script>
<script src="http://maxcdn.bootstrapcdn.com/bootstrap/3.3.5/js/bootstrap.min.js"></script>
</head>
<body>
<div class="container">
<h2>Justified Button Groups in Bootstrap</h2>
```

```html
<div class="btn-group btn-group-justified">
<div class="btn-group">
<button type="button" class="btnbtn-primary">Windows</button>
</div>
<div class="btn-group">
<button type="button" class="btnbtn-primary">Linux</button>
</div>
<div class="btn-group">
<button type="button" class="btnbtn-primary">OS X</button>
</div>
</div>
</body>
</html>
```

Just write the above program as it has been written, and then run it. You will observe the following as the output:

Justified Button Groups in Bootstrap

| Windows | Linux | OS X |

Notice how the elements have been wrapped into a button group in the above case.

Nesting of Dropdown & Menus Button Groups

When button groups have been nested, dropdown menus are created. Consider the example given below:

```html
<!DOCTYPE html>
<html lang="en">
<head>
<title>Bootstrap sample code</title>
<meta charset="utf-8">
<meta name="viewport" content="width=device-width, initial-scale=1">
<link rel="stylesheet" href="http://maxcdn.bootstrapcdn.com/bootstrap/3.3.5/css/bootstrap.min.css">
```

```html
<script src="https://ajax.googleapis.com/ajax/libs/jquery/1.11.3/jquery.min.js"></script>
<script src="http://maxcdn.bootstrapcdn.com/bootstrap/3.3.5/js/bootstrap.min.js"></script>
</head>
<body>
<div class="container">
<h2>Nesting of Button Groups</h2>
<p>When button groups have been nested, dropdown menus are created:</p>
<div class="btn-group">
<button type="button" class="btnbtn-primary">Windows</button>
<button type="button" class="btnbtn-primary">OS X</button>
<div class="btn-group">
<button type="button" class="btnbtn-primary dropdown-toggle" data-toggle="dropdown">
Linux<span class="caret"></span></button>
```

```
<ul class="dropdown-menu" role="menu">
<li><a href="#">Red Hat</a></li>
<li><a href="#">Cent OS </a></li>
                              </ul>
</div>
</div>
</div>
</body>
</html>
```

Just write the above program as it has been written, and then run it. You will observe the following as the output:

Just click on the drop down for Linux, and observe the options that you will be presented with. These should be the ones that you have specified. These are shown in the figure given below:

Nesting of Button Groups

When button groups have been nested, dropdown menus are created:

You have nowLEARNED how to create a dropdown by nesting your button groups in Bootstrap.

Split Button Groups

An example of this is given in the code shown below:

```
<!DOCTYPE html>
<html lang="en">
<head>
<title>Bootstrap sample code</title>
<meta charset="utf-8">
<meta name="viewport" content="width=device-width, initial-scale=1">
```

```html
<link rel="stylesheet" href="http://maxcdn.bootstrapcdn.com/bootstrap/3.3.5/css/bootstrap.min.css">
<script src="https://ajax.googleapis.com/ajax/libs/jquery/1.11.3/jquery.min.js"></script>
<script src="http://maxcdn.bootstrapcdn.com/bootstrap/3.3.5/js/bootstrap.min.js"></script>
</head>
<body>
<div class="container">
<h2>Split Buttons in Bootstrap</h2>
<div class="btn-group">
<button type="button" class="btnbtn-primary">Linux</button>
<button type="button" class="btnbtn-primary dropdown-toggle" data-toggle="dropdown">
<span class="caret"></span>
</button>
<ul class="dropdown-menu" role="menu">
```

```html
<li><a href="#">Cent OS</a></li>
<li><a href="#">Red Hat</a></li>
</ul>
</div>
</div>
</body>
</html>
```

Just write the program as it has been written above, and then run it. The following will be observed as the output from it:

Split Buttons in Bootstrap

Linux ▼

You can click on the dropdown arrow, and then observe the choices that you get. They should be as follows:

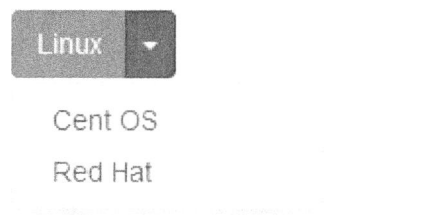

Chapter 9- Glyphicons in Bootstrap

In Bootstrap, there are over 200 glyphicons which can be added from the Glaphiconshalflings set. One can use glyphicons in text, toolbars, buttons, forms, navigations, and others. There are various glyphicons which are provided, such as the ones for download, search, message, and print. Consider the following example which demonstrates how these can be implemented in Bootstrap:

```
<!DOCTYPE html>
<html lang="en">
<head>
<title>Bootstrap sample code</title>
```

```html
<meta charset="utf-8">
<meta name="viewport" content="width=device-width, initial-scale=1">
<link rel="stylesheet" href="http://maxcdn.bootstrapcdn.com/bootstrap/3.3.5/css/bootstrap.min.css">
<script src="https://ajax.googleapis.com/ajax/libs/jquery/1.11.3/jquery.min.js"></script>
<script src="http://maxcdn.bootstrapcdn.com/bootstrap/3.3.5/js/bootstrap.min.js"></script>
</head>
<body>
<div class="container">
<h2>Glyphiconsamples</h2>
<p>Envelope icon: <span class="glyphiconglyphicon-envelope"></span></p>
<p>Envelope icon implemented as a link:
```

```html
<a href="#"><span class="glyphiconglyphicon-envelope"></span></a>
</p>
<p>Search icon: <span class="glyphiconglyphicon-search"></span></p>
<p>The Search icon added on a button:
<button type="button" class="btnbtn-default">
<span class="glyphiconglyphicon-search"></span> Search
</button>
</p>
<p>The Search icon added on a styled button:
<button type="button" class="btnbtn-info">
<span class="glyphiconglyphicon-search"></span> Search
</button>
</p>
```

```html
<p>Print icon: <span class="glyphiconglyphicon-print"></span></p>
<p>The Print icon added on a styled link button:
<a href="#" class="btnbtn-success btn-lg">
<span class="glyphiconglyphicon-print"></span> Print
</a>
</p>
</div>
</body>
</html>
```

Just write the above program as it has been written, and then run it. The following output will be observed:

Glyphicon samples

Envelope icon: ✉

Envelope icon implemented as a link: ✉

Search icon: 🔍

The Search icon added on a button: 🔍 Search

The Search icon added on a styled button:

Print icon: 🖨

The Print icon added on a styled link button: 🖨 Print

Chapter 10- Badges and Labels in Bootstrap

Badges

Badges are indicators in numerical form which show the number of items which are associated with a particular link. To create badges, one has to use the class ".badge" which should be placed within the element "<span>" and the badge will be created.

Consider the example given below:

```
<!DOCTYPE html>
<html lang="en">
<head>
<title>Bootstrap sample code</title>
<meta charset="utf-8">
```

```html
<meta name="viewport" content="width=device-width, initial-scale=1">
<link rel="stylesheet" href="http://maxcdn.bootstrapcdn.com/bootstrapBootstrap/3.3.5/css/bootstrap.min.css">
<script src="https://ajax.googleapis.com/ajax/libs/jquery/1.11.3/jquery.min.js"></script>
<script src="http://maxcdn.bootstrapcdn.com/bootstrap/3.3.5/js/bootstrap.min.js"></script>
</head>
<body>
<div class="container">
<h2>Example Badges</h2>
<a href="#">Expert users<span class="badge">5</span></a><br>
<a href="#">Novice users<span class="badge">10</span></a><br>
<a href="#">Intermediate users <span class="badge">10</span></a><br>
```

```
</div>
</body>
</html>
```

Just write the above program as it has been written, and then run it. The following output will be observed from it:

Example Badges

Expert users 5
Novice users 10
Intermediate users 10

Note that the numbers 5, 10, and 10 are the badges. The blue text is the link and each has an associated number which shows the number of users belonging to the link.

Other than adding them to links, badges can also be added to the other elements inline such as the buttons. Consider the example given below:

<!DOCTYPE html>

```html
<html lang="en">
<head>
<title>Bootstrap sample code</title>
<meta charset="utf-8">
<meta name="viewport" content="width=device-width, initial-scale=1">
<link rel="stylesheet" href="http://maxcdn.bootstrapcdn.com/bootstrap/3.3.5/css/bootstrap.min.css">
<script src="https://ajax.googleapis.com/ajax/libs/jquery/1.11.3/jquery.min.js"></script>
<script src="http://maxcdn.bootstrapcdn.com/bootstrap/3.3.5/js/bootstrap.min.js"></script>
</head>
<body>
<div class="container">
<h2>Badges added on Buttons</h2>
```

```
<button type="button" class="btnbtn-primary">Primary <span class="badge">10</span></button>
<button type="button" class="btnbtn-danger">Danger <span class="badge">2</span></button>
<button type="button" class="btnbtn-success">Success <span class="badge">8</span></button>
</div>
</body>
</html>
```

Just write the above program as it has been written, and then run it. The following output will be observed:

As shown in the above figure representing the output, the badges have been placed inline ON the button. This can also be applied to other elements belonging to Bootstrap.

Labels

With labels, additional information about something can be provided to the users. For one to add labels, the class ".label" must be used, and then followed by some other contextual classes which you will be shown in this section.

Consider the following example, which shows how labels can be created:

```
<!DOCTYPE html>
<html lang="en">
<head>
<title>Bootstrap sample code</title>
<meta charset="utf-8">
```

```html
<meta name="viewport" content="width=device-width, initial-scale=1">
<link rel="stylesheet" href="http://maxcdn.bootstrapcdn.com/bootstrap/3.3.5/css/bootstrap.min.css">
<script src="https://ajax.googleapis.com/ajax/libs/jquery/1.11.3/jquery.min.js"></script>
<script src="http://maxcdn.bootstrapcdn.com/bootstrap/3.3.5/js/bootstrap.min.js"></script>
</head>
<body>
<div class="container">
<h2>Labels in Bootstrap</h2>
<h1>Student 1<span class="label label-default">New</span></h1>
<h2> Student 2<span class="label label-default">New</span></h2>
<h3> Student2 <span class="label label-default">New</span></h3>
```

```html
<h4> Student2 <span class="label label-default">New</span></h4>
<h5> Student2 <span class="label label-default">New</span></h5>
<h6> Student2 <span class="label label-default">New</span></h6>
</div>
</body>
</html>
```

Just write the above program as it has been written, and then run it. The following output will be observed from it:

Labels in Bootstrap

Student 1 New

Student 2 New

Student 2 New

Student 2 New

Student 2 New

Student 2 New

This shows how the labels have been added to your text, and the user will be in a position to inquire more from them.

We earlier on talked of the classes which are used together with the ".label" class. These are commonly referred to as contextual classes, and they are shown in the code given below:

```
<!DOCTYPE html>
<html lang="en">
<head>
```

```html
<title>Bootstrap sample code</title>
<meta charset="utf-8">
<meta name="viewport" content="width=device-width, initial-scale=1">
<link rel="stylesheet" href="http://maxcdn.bootstrapcdn.com/bootstrap/3.3.5/css/bootstrap.min.css">
<script src="https://ajax.googleapis.com/ajax/libs/jquery/1.11.3/jquery.min.js"></script>
<script src="http://maxcdn.bootstrapcdn.com/bootstrap/3.3.5/js/bootstrap.min.js"></script>
</head>
<body>
<div class="container">
<h2>Contextual Label Classes</h2>
<p>Whenever you need to color your label, use the label contextual classes.</p>
<span class="label label-success">Success Label</span>
```

```html
<span class="label label-default">Default Label</span>
<span class="label label-info">Info Label</span>
<span class="label label-primary">Primary Label</span>
<span class="label label-warning">Warning Label</span>
<span class="label label-danger">Danger Label</span>
</div>
</body>
</html>
```

Just write the above program as it has been written, and then run it. You will observe the following as its output:

Contextual Label Classes

Whenever you need to color your label, use the label contextual classes.

Success Label Default Label Info Label Primary Label Warning Label Danger Label

Chapter 11- Progress Bars in Bootstrap

With progress bars, how far the user has progressed in doing a particular task can be shown. There are several types of progress bars in Bootstrap.

In case you want to create a default progress bar, you add the class ".progress" to the "<div>" element. This is shown in the example given below:

```
<!DOCTYPE html>
<html lang="en">
<head>
<title>Bootstrap sample code</title>
<meta charset="utf-8">
<meta name="viewport" content="width=device-width, initial-scale=1">
```

```html
<link rel="stylesheet" href="http://maxcdn.bootstrapcdn.com/bootstrap/3.3.5/css/bootstrap.min.css">
<script src="https://ajax.googleapis.com/ajax/libs/jquery/1.11.3/jquery.min.js"></script>
<script src="http://maxcdn.bootstrapcdn.com/bootstrap/3.3.5/js/bootstrap.min.js"></script>
</head>
<body>
<div class="container">
<h2>A Basic Progress Bar in Bootstrap</h2>
<div class="progress">
<div class="progress-bar" role="progressbar" aria-valuenow="70" aria-valuemin="0" aria-valuemax="100" style="width:60%">
<span class="sr-only">60% Complete</span>
</div>
</div>
</div>
</body>
```

</html>

Just write the above program as it has been written, and then run it. The following output will be observed from it:

A Basic Progress Bar in Bootstrap

Note that if you are using Internet Explorer 9 and above, then progress bars will not be supported, as they are made in CSS3 transitions.

Progress bar having a Label

We now need to demonstrate how a label can be added to a progress bar. The label can be used as an indication of the percentage that the progress bar has completed. If you need to make the label on the progress bar visible, then the class ".sr-only" must be removed from your code. Consider the example given below, which shows how this can be implemented:

```html
<!DOCTYPE html>
<html lang="en">
<head>
<title>Bootstrap sample code</title>
<meta charset="utf-8">
<meta name="viewport" content="width=device-width, initial-scale=1">
<link rel="stylesheet" href="http://maxcdn.bootstrapcdn.com/bootstrap/3.3.5/css/bootstrap.min.css">
<script src="https://ajax.googleapis.com/ajax/libs/jquery/1.11.3/jquery.min.js"></script>
<script src="http://maxcdn.bootstrapcdn.com/bootstrap/3.3.5/js/bootstrap.min.js"></script>
</head>
<body>
<div class="container">
<h2>Progress Bar having a Label</h2>
```

```html
<div class="progress">
<div class="progress-bar" role="progressbar"
aria-valuenow="60" aria-valuemin="0" aria-
valuemax="100" style="width:60%">
60%
</div>
</div>
</div>
</body>
</html>
```

Just write the above program as it has been written, and then run it. The following output will be observed:

Progress Bar having a Label

60%

As shown in the above figure representing the output, the width of the bar is 60%, and the same value has also been shown on it as the label. This will help in increasing the understanding of the user in terms of the percentage that their task has completed.

Progress bars with colors

When one wants to add meaning by the use of color to their progress bars, then there are contextual classes which can be used for this purpose.

Consider the example given below, which shows how different contextual classes can be used for this purpose:

```
<!DOCTYPE html>
<html lang="en">
                                <head>
<title>Bootstrap sample code</title>
<meta charset="utf-8">
```

```html
<meta name="viewport" content="width=device-width, initial-scale=1">
<link rel="stylesheet" href="http://maxcdn.bootstrapcdn.com/bootstrap/3.3.5/css/bootstrap.min.css">
<script src="https://ajax.googleapis.com/ajax/libs/jquery/1.11.3/jquery.min.js"></script>
<script src="http://maxcdn.bootstrapcdn.com/bootstrap/3.3.5/js/bootstrap.min.js"></script>
</head>
<body>
<div class="container">
<h2>Progress Bars with Colors</h2>
<p>We can color progress bars by use of contextual classes:</p>
<div class="progress">
```

```html
<div class="progress-bar progress-bar-success" role="progressbar" aria-valuenow="30" aria-valuemin="0" aria-valuemax="100" style="width:30%">
30% Complete (success)
</div>
</div>
<div class="progress">
<div class="progress-bar progress-bar-info" role="progressbar" aria-valuenow="40" aria-valuemin="0" aria-valuemax="100" style="width:40%">
40% Complete (info)
</div>
</div>
<div class="progress">
<div class="progress-bar progress-bar-warning" role="progressbar" aria-valuenow="50" aria-valuemin="0" aria-valuemax="100" style="width:50%">
50% Complete (warning)
</div>
```

```
</div>
<div class="progress">
<div class="progress-bar progress-bar-danger" role="progressbar" aria-valuenow="60" aria-valuemin="0" aria-valuemax="100" style="width:60%">
60% Complete (danger)
</div>
</div>
</div>
</body>
</html>
```

Just write the above program as it has been written, and then run it. The following output will be observed from it:

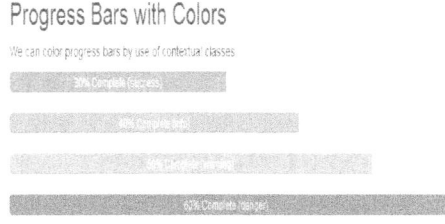

Note that each of the bars has a different color, a different width, and a different and unique label. That is how we can add colors to our progress bars.

Progress Bars with stripes

It is possible for us to add stripes to our progress bars. This can be done by the use of the class ".progress-bar-striped."

Consider the example given below, which shows how this can be implemented:

```
<!DOCTYPE html>
<html lang="en">
<head>
<title>Bootstrap sample code</title>
<meta charset="utf-8">
<meta name="viewport" content="width=device-width, initial-scale=1">
```

```html
<link rel="stylesheet" href="http://maxcdn.bootstrapcdn.com/bootstrap/3.3.5/css/bootstrap.min.css">
<script src="https://ajax.googleapis.com/ajax/libs/jquery/1.11.3/jquery.min.js"></script>
<script src="http://maxcdn.bootstrapcdn.com/bootstrap/3.3.5/js/bootstrap.min.js"></script>
</head>
<body>
<div class="container">
<h2> Progress Bars with Stripes</h2>
<p>The class .progress-bar-striped can be used to add stripes to the progress bars:</p>
<div class="progress">
<div class="progress-bar progress-bar-success progress-bar-striped" role="progressbar" aria-valuenow="30" aria-valuemin="0" aria-valuemax="100" style="width:30%">
30% Complete (success)
```

```html
    </div>
  </div>
  <div class="progress">
    <div class="progress-bar progress-bar-info progress-bar-striped" role="progressbar" aria-valuenow="40" aria-valuemin="0" aria-valuemax="100" style="width:40%">
      40% Complete (info)
    </div>
  </div>
  <div class="progress">
    <div class="progress-bar progress-bar-warning progress-bar-striped" role="progressbar" aria-valuenow="50" aria-valuemin="0" aria-valuemax="100" style="width:50%">
      50% Complete (warning)
    </div>
  </div>
  <div class="progress">
```

```
<div class="progress-bar progress-bar-danger progress-bar-striped"
role="progressbar" aria-valuenow="60" aria-valuemin="0" aria-valuemax="100"
style="width:60%">
60% Complete (danger)
</div>
</div>
</div>
</body>
</html>
```

Just write the above as it has been written, and then run it. You will observe the following output:

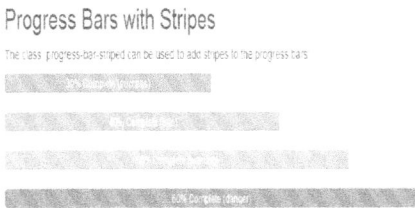

Note the stripes which are shown in the above progress bars.

Progress Bars with Animation

An animation effect can be added to our progress bars. This can be done by use of the class ".active."Consider the following example which shows how this can be implemented in Bootstrap:

```
<!DOCTYPE html>
<html lang="en">
<head>
<title> Bootstrap sample code </title>
<meta charset="utf-8">
<meta name="viewport" content="width=device-width, initial-scale=1">
<link rel="stylesheet" href="http://maxcdn.bootstrapcdn.com/bootstrap/3.3.5/css/bootstrap.min.css">
<script src="https://ajax.googleapis.com/ajax/libs/jquery/1.11.3/jquery.min.js"></script>
```

```html
<script src="http://maxcdn.bootstrapcdn.com/bootstrap/3.3.5/js/bootstrap.min.js"></script>
</head>
<body>
<div class="container">
<h2> Progress Bar with Animation </h2>
<p>The class .active can be used to animate the progress bar:</p>
<div class="progress">
<div class="progress-bar progress-bar-striped active" role="progressbar" aria-valuenow="80" aria-valuemin="0" aria-valuemax="100" style="width:80%">
80%
</div>
</div>
</div>
</body>
</html>
```

Just write the above program as it has been written, and then run it. You will observe the following as its output:

When you observe the output that you get after running the code, you will
notice that the blue color together with the stripes are in animation. That is how these can be implemented.

Stacked Progress Bars

This just means more than one progress bars joined together. If you need to implement these, just place them inside the "<div class="progress">" element.

Consider the example given below, showing how this can be implemented in Bootstrap:

```
<!DOCTYPE html>
<html lang="en">
```

```html
<head>
<title>Bootstrap sample code</title>
<meta charset="utf-8">
<meta name="viewport" content="width=device-width, initial-scale=1">
<link rel="stylesheet" href="http://maxcdn.bootstrapcdn.com/bootstrap/3.3.5/css/bootstrap.min.css">
<script src="https://ajax.googleapis.com/ajax/libs/jquery/1.11.3/jquery.min.js"></script>
<script src="http://maxcdn.bootstrapcdn.com/bootstrap/3.3.5/js/bootstrap.min.js"></script>
</head>
<body>
<div class="container">
<h2>Stacked Progress Bars in Bootstrap</h2>
```

<p>to create stacked progress bars, just place them into the same div with the .progress class:</p>
<div class="progress">
<div class="progress-bar progress-bar-success" role="progressbar" style="width:50%">
Free Space
</div>
<div class="progress-bar progress-bar-warning" role="progressbar" style="width:10%">
Warning
</div>
<div class="progress-bar progress-bar-danger" role="progressbar" style="width:20%">
Danger
</div>
</div>
</div>
</body>

</html>

Just write the above program as it has been written, and then run it. You will observe the following output:

As shown in the above figure, the bars have been stacked together, and for one to differentiate them, they must use either their unique colors or width.

Chapter 12- The Tooltip plugin in Bootstrap

The tooltip just means the pop up which is seen after the user has moved the mouse pointer, and especially over a particular element.

To create this, the attribute "data-toggle="tooltip"" has to be added to the element. You can then use the attribute *"title"* so as to indicate the text which is expected to appear in the tooltip. This is shown below:

```
<a href="#" data-toggle="tooltip" title="Hooray!">This is the tooltip text</a>
```

To indicate a ttoltip, jQuery must be used. Consider the example given below:

```
<!DOCTYPE html>
<html lang="en">
```

```html
<head>
<title>Bootstrap sample code </title>
<meta charset="utf-8">
<meta name="viewport" content="width=device-width, initial-scale=1">
<link rel="stylesheet" href="http://maxcdn.bootstrapcdn.com/bootstrap/3.3.5/css/bootstrap.min.css">
<script src="https://ajax.googleapis.com/ajax/libs/jquery/1.11.3/jquery.min.js"></script>
<script src="http://maxcdn.bootstrapcdn.com/bootstrap/3.3.5/js/bootstrap.min.js"></script>
</head>
<body>
<div class="container">
<h3>A Tooltip Example</h3>
<a href="#" data-toggle="tooltip" title="Hello there!">Just hover me and observe</a>
</div>
```

```
<script>
$(document).ready(function(){
$(document).ready(function(){
$('[data-toggle="tooltip"]').tooltip();
});
</script>
</body>
</html>
```

Just write the above program as it has been written, and then run it. The following output will be observed:

A Tooltip Example
Just hover me and observe

You can then move the cursor over the text with color, and then observe what happens. You should see some text labeled *"Hello there!"* which is the tooltip title.

Conclusion

It can be concluded that Bootstrap is a very important and useful framework for the development of web applications. It is used by programmers to create web pages which respond automatically on devices with different screen sizes so that there is not a noticeable change in the layout of these pages. This is done by the use of the grid system which is supported in Bootstrap. Note that a maximum of 12 columns is supported per each row in Bootstrap. If you exceed this, then you will get an error. When it comes to images, they can be implemented or added differently in Bootstrap. For instance, one can choose that their images should have round corners or the images can be circular. An image gallery can also be created with Bootstrap, and links added to each of the images in the gallery.

These have all been discussed in this book. One can also choose to add some effects to their text which is to appear in their web pages, and this makes the web pages become attractive to users. Bootstrap also supports alerts. These are used to attract attention from the users for an important task. Animations and other effects which can be added to these have been discussed in this book. To make it easy for users to understand what they are doing, elements such as glyphicons can be used. Progress bars, which help the users to understand how far they have gone in performing their work are very important. You need to know how to implement these, and add some effects to them. You also need to understand how elements such as badges and labels can be implemented, as they are very helpful to users. My hope is that this book has helped you in understanding these.

Made in the USA
Monee, IL
06 February 2021